2ND EDITION

CHRISTMAS

ARRANGED BY ERIC BAUMGARTNER

ISBN 978-1-70510-297-8

EXCLUSIVELY DISTRIBUTED BY

WILLIS MUSIC · HAL•LEONARD®

© 2000, 2020 by The Willis Music Co.
International Copyright Secured   All Rights Reserved

Visit Hal Leonard Online at
www.halleonard.com

Contact us:
Hal Leonard
7777 West Bluemound Road
Milwaukee, WI 53213
Email: info@halleonard.com

In Europe, contact:
Hal Leonard Europe Limited
42 Wigmore Street
Marylebone, London, W1U 2RN
Email: info@halleonardeurope.com

In Australia, contact:
Hal Leonard Australia Pty. Ltd.
4 Lentara Court
Cheltenham, Victoria, 3192 Australia
Email: info@halleonard.com.au

PREFACE

Welcome to the 2nd edition of *Jazz It Up Christmas*! The original edition, published in 2000, was one of my very first publications for Willis Music and remains a favorite of mine. I still regularly perform the pieces for workshops, parties, and even the occasional church service! I am pleased that the original book has also remained a favorite with students, teachers, and gigging pianists. I was therefore quite enthusiastic about the prospect of working on a new expanded edition.

This new edition offers up six brand new pieces in addition to the original six. I found the experience of creating the new pieces just as enjoyable as creating the originals. The goal of a jazz arranger is to breathe new life into familiar songs through inventive melodic, harmonic, and rhythmic variation. I wanted to also capture the spirit and variety of the originals, so that the pieces form a cohesive musical program. In fact, the titles have been carefully sequenced to contrast and complement one another, just as would be done when programming a live performance. But of course each performer has the freedom to approach the pieces in any sequence they desire! It is my sincere hope that you have as much fun playing these pieces as I had in creating them.

PERFORMANCE NOTES (from the original edition). It is not essential for the player to have had previous jazz experience in order to learn and perform these pieces successfully; they are fully arranged. There are no chord symbols or sections requiring improvisation. The experienced jazz player, however, is welcome to experiment with rhythmic and melodic variation or "open up" various sections for improvisation. As for the less experienced "jazzer," this collection may serve as an introduction to the rhythmic, melodic, and harmonic vocabulary of jazz, and hopefully spark a desire for more in-depth study. Enjoy!

Eric Baumgartner

Angels We Have Heard on High

Traditional French Carol
Arranged by Eric Baumgartner

Allegretto

Relaxed Swing

Bring a Torch, Jeannette, Isabella

17th Century French Provençal Carol
Arranged by Eric Baumgartner

Slowly, mysteriously

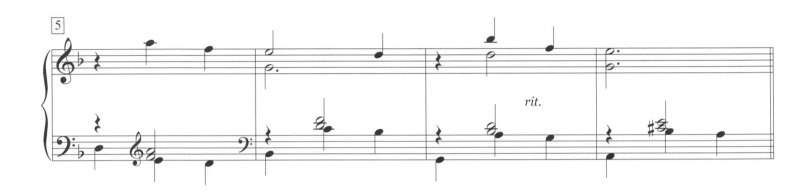

Deck the Hall

Traditional Welsh Carol
Arranged by Eric Baumgartner

Relaxed Blues/Swing tempo

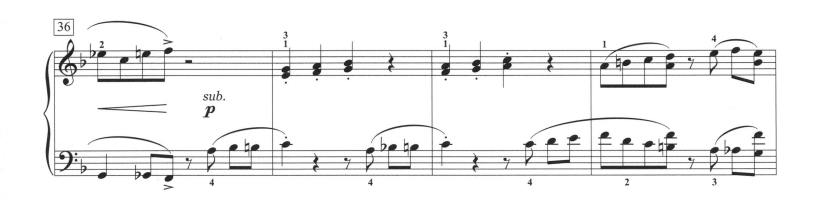

O Christmas Tree

Traditional German Carol
Arranged by Eric Baumgartner

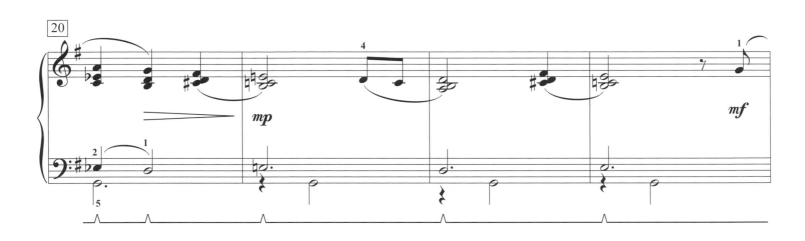

God Rest Ye Merry, Gentlemen

19th Century English Carol
Arranged by Eric Baumgartner

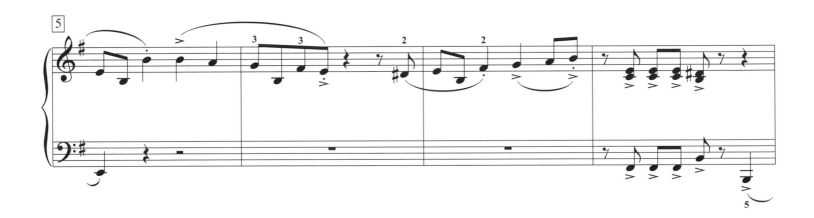

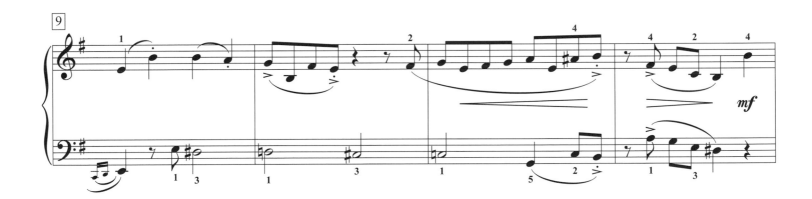

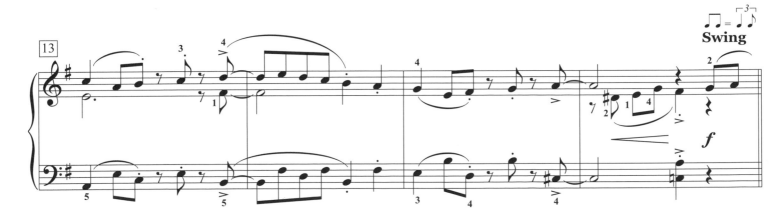

Ukrainian Bell Carol

Traditional
Music by Mykola Leontovych
Arranged by Eric Baumgartner

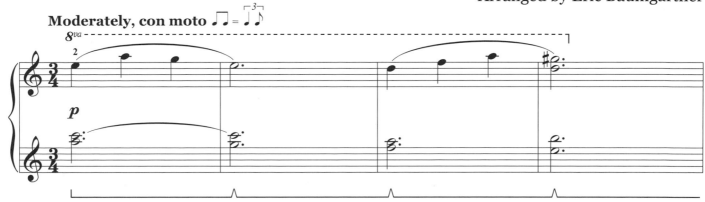

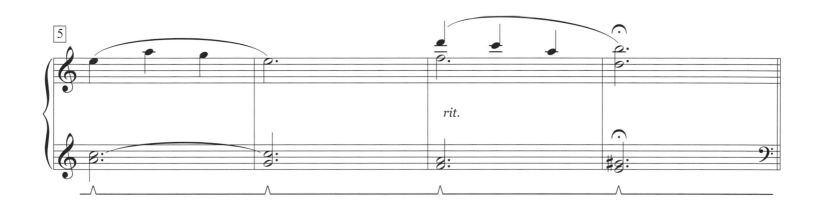

(continue light pedaling)

Good King Wenceslas

Music from *Piae Cantiones*
Arranged by Eric Baumgartner

Jesu, Joy of Man's Desiring

Johann Sebastian Bach
Arranged by Eric Baumgartner

With light pedal

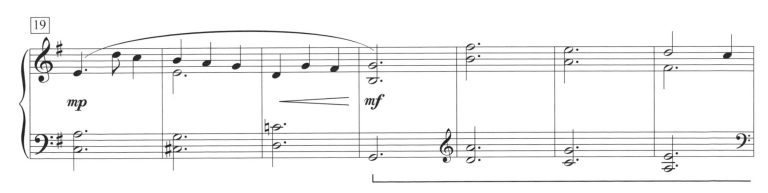

Coventry Carol

Traditional English Melody
Arranged by Eric Baumgartner

March

from THE NUTCRACKER SUITE, OP. 71A

Pyotr Il'yich Tchaikovsky
Arranged by Eric Baumgartner

Here We Come A-Caroling

Traditional
Arranged by Eric Baumgartner

Jingle Bells

Words and Music by J. Pierpont
Arranged by Eric Baumgartner

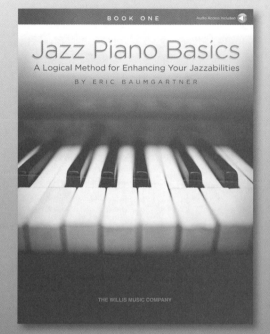

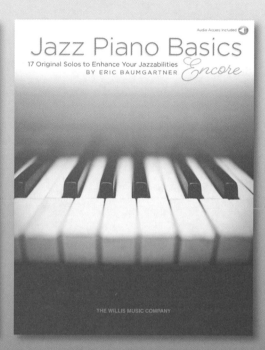

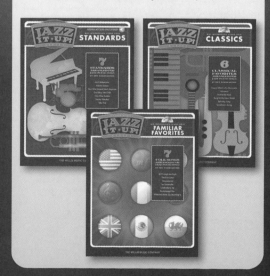

COMPOSER'S CHOICE

The Composer's Choice series showcases piano works by an exclusive group of composers, all of whom are also teachers and performers. Each collection contains 8 original solos and includes classic piano pieces that were carefully chosen by the composer, as well as brand-new compositions written especially for the series. The composers also contributed helpful and valuable performance notes for each collection. Get to know a new Willis composer today!

CLOSER LOOK

View sample pages and hear audio excerpts online at
www.halleonard.com

 @WillisPianoMusic

 willispiano

 @WillisPiano

 Willis Piano Music

WILLIS MUSIC

EXCLUSIVELY DISTRIBUTED BY
HAL•LEONARD®
www.willispianomusic.com
Prices, contents, and availability subject to change without notice.

ELEMENTARY

GLENDA AUSTIN
MID TO LATER ELEMENTARY
Betcha-Can Boogie • Jivin' Around • The Plucky Penguin • Rolling Clouds • Shadow Tag • Southpaw Swing • Sunset Over the Sea • Tarantella (Spider at Midnight).
00130168 ....$6.99

CAROLYN MILLER
MID TO LATER ELEMENTARY
The Goldfish Pool • March of the Gnomes • More Fireflies • Morning Dew • Ping Pong • The Piper's Dance • Razz-a-ma-tazz • Rolling River.
00118951 ....$7.99

CAROLYN C. SETLIFF
EARLY TO LATER ELEMENTARY
Dark and Stormy Night • Dreamland • Fantastic Fingers • Peanut Brittle • Six Silly Geese • Snickerdoodle • Roses in Twilight • Seahorse Serenade.
00119289 ....$7.99

INTERMEDIATE

GLENDA AUSTIN
EARLY TO MID-INTERMEDIATE
Blue Mood Waltz • Chromatic Conversation • Etude in E Major • Midnight Caravan • Reverie • South Sea Lullaby • Tangorific • Valse Belle.
00115242 ....$9.99

ERIC BAUMGARTNER
EARLY TO MID-INTERMEDIATE
Aretta's Rhumba • Beale Street Boogie • The Cuckoo • Goblin Dance • Jackrabbit Ramble • Journey's End • New Orleans Nocturne • Scherzando.
00114465 ....$9.99

RANDALL HARTSELL
EARLY TO MID-INTERMEDIATE
Above the Clouds • Autumn Reverie • Raiders in the Night • River Dance • Showers at Daybreak • Sunbursts in the Rain • Sunset in Madrid • Tides of Tahiti.
00122211 ....$8.99

NAOKO IKEDA
EARLY TO MID-INTERMEDIATE
Arigato • The Glacial Mermaid • Land of the Midnight Sun • Sakura • Scarlet Hearts (solo version) • Shooting Stars in Summer • Soft Rain (Azisai) • ...You.
00288891 ....$8.99

CAROLYN MILLER
EARLY INTERMEDIATE
Allison's Song • Little Waltz in E Minor • Reflections • Ripples in the Water • Arpeggio Waltz • Trumpet in the Night • Toccata Semplice • Rhapsody in A Minor.
00123897 ....$8.99